DARK BROWN

A Melodrama
in One Act

by
PHILIP JOHNSON

Illustrated by
ANTHONY MENDLESON

SAMUEL FRENCH

LONDON
NEW YORK SYDNEY TORONTO HOLLYWOOD

Copyright © 1976 By Samuel French Ltd
All Rights Reserved

DARK BROWN is fully protected under the copyright laws of the British Commonwealth, including Canada, the United States of America, and all other countries of the Copyright Union. All rights, including professional and amateur stage productions, recitation, lecturing, public reading, motion picture, radio broadcasting, television and the rights of translation into foreign languages are strictly reserved.

ISBN 978-0-573-02044-5

www.samuelfrench.co.uk
www.samuelfrench.com

FOR AMATEUR PRODUCTION ENQUIRIES

UNITED KINGDOM AND WORLD EXCLUDING NORTH AMERICA

plays@samuelfrench.co.uk

020 7255 4302/01

Each title is subject to availability from Samuel French, depending upon country of performance.

CAUTION: Professional and amateur producers are hereby warned that DARK BROWN is subject to a licensing fee. Publication of this play does not imply availability for performance. Both amateurs and professionals considering a production are strongly advised to apply to the appropriate agent before starting rehearsals, advertising, or booking a theatre. A licensing fee must be paid whether the title is presented for charity or gain and whether or not admission is charged.

The professional rights in this play are controlled by Samuel French Ltd, 52 Fitzroy Street, London, W1T 5JR.

No one shall make any changes in this title for the purpose of production. No part of this book may be reproduced, stored in a retrieval system, or transmitted in any form, by any means, now known or yet to be invented, including mechanical, electronic, photocopying, recording, videotaping, or otherwise, without the prior written permission of the publisher. No one shall upload this title, or part of this title, to any social media websites.

The right of Philip Johnson to be identified as author of this work has been asserted in accordance with Section 77 of the Copyright, Designs and Patents Act 1988.

CHARACTERS

Mrs. Collins.
Miss Tasker.
Jenny Brown.
Bella Crewe.
Fred Whitworth.
Mrs. Persophelous.
Arthur Brown.

The play happens in the living-room at the back of Arthur Brown's tobacconist shop, in a small town not far from London, on the evening of a summer's day, towards the end of the last century.

N.B.—All stage directions are given from the point of view of the actor.

DARK BROWN

The SCENE *is the living-room at the back of* ARTHUR BROWN'S *tobacconist shop in the High Street of a town not so very far from London, on the evening of a summer's day, towards the end of the last century.*

Up R., *in the back wall, is a door which, when open, reveals a little passage leading into the shop, which is off* R. *In the middle of the* R. *wall is a window, which is open, looking out on to a small yard with a high wall. Lace curtains looped back with satin ribbon drape the window, the whole being framed by other curtains of a dark maroon colour. The fireplace is in the* L. *wall, and above this is a door leading to the rest of the house. The furnishing is of course of the style affected during the last decade of the eighteen hundreds. Immediately beneath the window is a sofa. Above this is a small bamboo table on tripod legs, and upon which some sort of plant or fern is growing in a pot. Slightly to* L. *of the centre—rather nearer to the fireplace than to the window—is a round table draped with a fringed cloth, and upon it a dome-shaped glass case of wax fruit and flowers. Above and* R. *of the table are stiff-backed chairs upholstered with stamped velvet. Just above the fireplace is a similarly upholstered easy chair. At* R.C., *about midway between the table and the sofa, and rather more up stage than either, is an armchair. This latter is upholstered in some bright colour, scarlet or blue, so that it strikes a definite note in the room. Against the back wall, in the space* L. *of the door, is a bureau, with stiff-backed chairs set against the wall on either side of it. Below the window,* R., *is a fairly tall cupboard. . . . There are several pictures on the walls, two or three plaques, a couple of Japanese fans, and a fretwork wall-bracket or two, supporting little vases. Upon the mantelshelf are a tall vase of pampas grass, two bronze equestrian figures, and a variety of knick-knacks. Upon the bureau are an inkstand and a framed photograph. And, of course, over each chair-back there hangs an antimacassar. There is a suggestion of overcrowding, though care must be taken not to hamper the movements of the actors.*

When the CURTAIN *rises, it is still broad daylight outside, but within the room, thanks to the high wall which directly faces the window, the dusk already appears to be gathering. It is obvious that at all times the room must strike a somewhat chill and sombre note. The one occupant is* MRS. COLLINS, *who, seated upon the sofa to catch the light, is studying a newspaper through a reading-glass. She is in the early sixties: a woman with no very definite characteristics, whom at a guess one might take to be the widow* of a lower middle-class tradesman—which is precisely what she is. She wears a black dress, full-skirted and tight-bodiced, and upon her head is a cap: a flat little affair of white lace, trimmed with a knot of violets. For a moment nothing happens. The reading-glass weaves to and fro, line by line. Then the door up R. opens, and MISS TASKER puts her head round it. MISS TASKER is somewhere in her thirties, soberly dressed, and with her hair piled high on her head.

MISS TASKER (*giving a delicate little cough*). H'm!
MRS. COLLINS (*with a little start*). Oh——
MISS TASKER (*opening the door wider—advancing a step into the room—speaking with a trace of that accent which we nowadays describe as "refaned"*). I'm so very sorry to intrude, Mrs. Collins, but I was wondering if I might have a word with Mrs. Brown.
MRS. COLLINS. My daughter's in the kitchen, Miss Tasker. (*Laying the paper and reading-glass beside her.*) I'll call her.
MISS TASKER (*moving down R. of the armchair*). No, no, please, I wouldn't do that! It's of no great consequence, really. I just thought she might happen to know where that special mixture is that Mr. Brown makes up for the Colonel, that's all. I can't seem to lay my hands on it, and he may call this evening.
MRS. COLLINS (*who has risen*). I see. Well, I'll go and fetch her, shall I?
MISS TASKER (*hastily*). No, no, really, I wouldn't! The Colonel's *very* obliging. I know he won't in the least mind having some other mixture, for once.
MRS. COLLINS. Well, if you really think . . .

And she is making queen cakes, and you know what queen cakes are, Miss Tasker.

Miss Tasker. Oh, quite, quite! And, anyway, Mr. Brown may be back before the Colonel calls. The last time he went to Eastbourne, he was back quite early, if you remember.

Mrs. Collins (*sitting again*). That was, let me see, a fortnight ago, wasn't it?

Miss Tasker. A fortnight last Tuesday, yes.

Mrs. Collins. That's it: a fortnight last Tuesday. And once the week before that, if I remember rightly.

Miss Tasker (*with a nod*). His poor auntie having taken one of her turns for the worse. (*Fetching a sigh.*) It's wonderful, really, how she recovers from those attacks, isn't it? She must have a quite remarkable constitution, when you come to think.

Mrs. Collins. And after being bedridden for fifteen years, what's more.

Miss Tasker. Really, though one scarcely likes to say it, it would be almost a mercy . . . if—you know what I mean . . .

Mrs. Collins. She certainly can't be getting much out of life. . . .

Miss Tasker. Mr. Brown must be a great comfort to her, popping over every now and then, mustn't he?

Mrs. Collins (*with just the faintest trace of something that is not altogether sincere in her tone*). Yes . . . I suppose he must.

Miss Tasker. And not just for an hour or so. Makes a real visit of it. Stays the night and comes back next day.

Mrs. Collins (*still in that same tone*). Oh, yes . . . Mr. Brown always stays the night when he goes to Eastbourne.

(*A short pause.* Mrs. Collins *takes up the paper and reading-glass from beside her.*)

Miss Tasker (*moving up* R.). Oh, well . . . (*Her hand on the door-handle—lingering.*) You don't find the light tries your eyes, Mrs. Collins? This is such a *very* dark room, don't you think?

Mrs. Collins. "Gloomy" is my word for it, Miss Tasker. I certainly couldn't live in it for always. . . . But I just wanted to read about the hanging.

Miss Tasker (*not quite catching the word*). The——?

Mrs. Collins. George Wainwright, the Sevenoaks murderer. They hanged him this morning at Pentonville, it says here.

Miss Tasker. Oh, I don't think I . . .

Mrs. Collins. You must have read about it, surely. A dreadful man. Kept a grocer's shop, all very respectable, and seemed as devoted as could be to his wife. But every now and then, he'd go away for a day or two——

Miss Tasker. Yes, now I remember. (*Moving down a little.*) To stay with his grandmother at Dover, wasn't it?

Mrs. Collins. Who was *supposed* to be ill. And then, if

you please, his poor wife finds out he hasn't even *got* a grandmother, ill or well——

MISS TASKER (*coming down* L. *of the sofa*). Wasn't it—a lady friend he was visiting all the time——

MRS. COLLINS. His fancy woman! And when his wife taxes him with it, he makes no more ado, but snatches a length of rope, and strangles her on the spot! Strangles her, if you please!

MISS TASKER (*with a shudder, moving below the easy chair*). Dreadful! (*One hand to her throat—shuddering again.*) Dreadful! (*Turning to face* MRS. COLLINS.) You'd wonder how any man *could*!

MRS. COLLINS. A good business, mind you, a loving wife, respected by everybody—and yet, behind it all, hidden away in the dark, a vile, cruel beast!

MISS TASKER. Hanging's too good, that's what I say! And to think there may be others like him in the world! Well, there may be, Mrs. Collins. I might pass one in the street any day, or—or serve him with tobacco over the counter. You never know, do you?

MRS. COLLINS (*after a moment's pause*). No, that's just what I was thinking, Miss Tasker . . . you never know.

MISS TASKER (*at* R.C., *below the chair, launching out upon what one feels is a favourite topic*). If you ask me, Mrs. Collins, *any* woman who trusts *any* man these days is a fool! (*Adding hastily.*) Not that there was anything wrong with Mr. Collins, I'm *quite* sure.

MRS. COLLINS. Well, I'll give him his due, he never tried to strangle me.

MISS TASKER. But as for most of them—well, being in a tobacconist shop I'm brought into contact, and I *know*! Some of 'em, I'm sure, can't ask for a half-ounce of twist without making you go hot all over! And the way they'll look at you, and try to touch your hand when you give them their change!

MRS. COLLINS (*clicking her tongue and shaking her head*). Tck! Tck! Tck! Disgusting!

MISS TASKER. Only last evening, now, a very flash-looking man—the sporting type, you know—had the impudence to say, "And what are you doing to-night, Miss?" And when I said, quick as lightning, "Going to bed," he made a remark which—well—I could *not* repeat.

MRS. COLLINS. Oh dear.

MISS TASKER. Quite uncalled for, as I told him to his face.

(*A short pause while they follow their respective trains of thought. Then :*)

(*Rallying herself.*) Oh, well, I'd better go and make sure the shop hasn't run away. (*Crossing up* R. *to the door.*) And don't worry Mrs. Brown about the Colonel's mixture. Mr. Brown may be back from Eastbourne any time now. . . . (*Turning at the door.*) You'd think he'd find the journey dull, wouldn't you, doing it so often ?

MRS. COLLINS. He certainly does the journey very often.

(*There is the sharp " ting " of a bell from the shop. This " ting " is heard at irregular intervals until the point in the play when the shop is closed.*)

MISS TASKER. There ! A customer ! Excuse me.

(*She goes out hurriedly, closing the door behind her.* MRS. COLLINS *does not immediately resume her reading. Instead, she looks first towards the door through which* MISS TASKER *has just departed, then towards the other door. Her expression, now that she is alone, has grown thoughtful, and faintly tinged with worry. She sits very still, then gives herself a little shake, starts to heave a sigh, checks the sigh, and picks up the reading-glass, as though to resume her reading. As she does so,* JENNY BROWN, *her daughter, comes in through the door up* L. JENNY *is twenty-seven; not beautiful; not pretty, even; but, in a quiet way,*

attractive. She is wearing a plain but pleasing dress of grey, trimmed with narrow bands of amethyst ribbon-velvet, and over it a white apron which she is untying as she enters.)

JENNY. There, thank goodness, that's done—and what's more, turned out light as a feather !

MRS. COLLINS. I'm glad. They're tricky things, queen cakes. I'm never sure they're worth the trouble, myself.

JENNY (*folding her apron*). Arthur likes them. And he never seems to have much of an appetite when he gets back from Eastbourne. He has to be tempted. (*She lays the folded apron on the arm of the easy chair.*)

MRS. COLLINS (*offering no comment on the subject of* ARTHUR'S *appetite—silent for a moment*). I thought that was your best dress, Jenny. Have you taken to it for weekdays now ?

JENNY (*picking an imaginary bit of fluff off the sleeve*). Not really, I just thought I'd put it on for when Arthur gets home.

His trips to Eastbourne seem to depress him, somehow. Takes him quite a day or so before he gets back to his usual self.

Mrs. Collins. Oh ?

Jenny. The last time, he just sat here all the evening, and scarcely uttered a word. If it had been anyone but Arthur, I'd have thought he'd got something on his mind.

Mrs. Collins (*dryly*). And, of course, Arthur could never have anything on *his* mind.

Jenny. Not without me knowing. (*Her mother remains silent—a shade defensively.*) After all, I can hardly expect him to come home merry as a lark, when he's been sitting for hours and hours with a bedridden invalid. It wouldn't be natural.

Mrs. Collins. No, dear. (*Shifting her position slightly.*) I wonder he never takes you with him to see his auntie. If she's so mortal fond of her nephew, you'd think she'd be anxious to meet his wife, wouldn't you ?

Jenny. He'd have taken me long ago ; but meeting strangers is bad for her : it excites her.

Mrs. Collins (*after just the faintest suspicion of a sniff*). Oh ? I'd have thought, after fifteen years in bed, she'd have welcomed a little excitement.

Jenny. Arthur says not. (*Looking round the room.*) Now, let me see . . . Oh, yes, the flowers !

(*She picks up the folded apron from the easy chair, and hurries out up* L. Mrs. Collins *sits quite still for a moment. Then, rising, she places her newspaper and reading-glass on the table, goes to the bureau and picks up the framed photograph. She studies the photograph intently, holding it first at almost arm's length, then much nearer, frowning slightly. Then she replaces it on the bureau. As she does so,* Jenny *re-enters, carrying a vase of flowers.*)

That's good of him, isn't it ? It's the one he had taken on our honeymoon, just over a year ago. (*She places the vase on the table.*)

Mrs. Collins (*going to the fireplace*). Ah ? . . . I suppose you don't know exactly what time he'll be back, Jenny ?

Jenny (*carrying the glass case of wax fruit to the bureau*). Not exactly. But he'll not be long now, I'm sure.

Mrs. Collins. I was thinking I'd like to get back to Clapham before dark, if I could.

Jenny (*returning to the table,* c.). But Cousin Bella and Fred are calling to take you home, Mother. They'll be here in plenty of time for that.

Mrs. Collins. Yes—*if* they've come down for the day. So long as I can catch the six-fifty. The seven-forty makes it so late.

JENNY (*coaxing the flowers into a better display of their charms*). You'll get the six-fifty all right. You've no distance to walk, with the station just down the street. This place is very convenient.

MRS. COLLINS. It may be . . . though I may as well say it as think it: this house would never suit *me*. No, thank you!

JENNY (*stepping back to admire the flowers*). Why, I'm sure it's a very good house, Mother!

MRS. COLLINS. I'm not saying it isn't well built . . .

JENNY. What's wrong with it, then? (*She sets the vase o. of the table.*)

MRS. COLLINS. I dunno. . . . It gives me a sort of feeling, Jenny.

JENNY. Feeling?

MRS. COLLINS. As though I was all cut off, and miles away from anywhere.

JENNY (*looking at her—then, with a little laugh*). But that's silly, Mother! Why, we're right in the very busiest part of the town.

MRS. COLLINS. I dare say. (*She sits in the armchair above the fire.*) All the same, I'm sure that last night, when the shop door was bolted and barred, and we were sitting in this room, I felt I was on top of a mountain, or in the middle of a wood—and I didn't like the feeling. I didn't like it at all.

JENNY. Why, I remember thinking how cosy it was, just the two of us.

MRS. COLLINS. I'd sooner wait for that sort of cosiness until I'm dead: I'll get plenty of it in the grave, I reckon.

JENNY (*a little hurt*). Oh, Mother, *what* a thing to say!

MRS. COLLINS. For one thing, Jenny, you can't say it's ever really *light* in this room, now can you?

JENNY. That's because it faces the yard wall. (*Crossing to the mantel.*) And even if it does make the room a bit dark, it keeps it private. (*She adjusts the dressing of the mantel.*)

MRS. COLLINS. It certainly does. It's so private, anything could happen. You might scream your head off, and there'd not be a soul to see or hear.

JENNY (*turning to face her*). Good heavens, Mother! There's no need to talk as if I was going to be murdered. (*Crossing R., below the table.*) Really, I can't think what's come over you!

MRS. COLLINS. Nothing's come over me.

(JENNY *turns at* R.O., *to listen.*)

I'm just saying, Jenny, it isn't the sort of home I'd have chosen for you, if I'd had *my* way.

JENNY. Well, it happens to be the place where Arthur has his tobacconist business—and a very good business, too, I may say. He's worked it up wonderfully since we came here. Another year or so, and it'll be a proper little gold-mine.

MRS. COLLINS (*in a falsely bright tone*). That's all right, then, isn't it ?

(JENNY *goes to the window and fiddles with the lace curtains, twitching the folds into position. There is a short pause. Then :*)

JENNY (*still choosing to be occupied with the curtains—broaching a subject she would have preferred to avoid*). The fact is—you don't like Arthur very much, do you, Mother ? (*She gives a final twitch at the curtains.*)

MRS. COLLINS (*after a second's pause—evasively*). I've never said I didn't like him.

JENNY (*turning from the window*). You don't have to. Every time his name's mentioned, you . . . close up.

MRS. COLLINS. I'm sure I don't know what you mean.

JENNY. Oh, yes, you do. (*Moving to* R. *of the table.*) And it isn't fair to him. There's lots worse men in the world than Arthur, you know.

MRS. COLLINS. I dare say. But when I married your father, it wasn't because there were lots worse, but because there were few better.

JENNY. But you've got nothing definite *against* Arthur ?

MRS. COLLINS. Not that I know of.

JENNY. Very well, then.

MRS. COLLINS. Except that he's old enough to be your father.

JENNY (*tartly—moving up to the bureau*). The fact is, Mother, you'd set your heart on me marrying Fred Whitworth, and you've never got over your disappointment. (*She opens a drawer as if about to get something out.*)

MRS. COLLINS. Fred Whitworth's a good, steady fellow, and I like him.

JENNY. So do I, if it comes to that.

MRS. COLLINS. *And* he was wild about you. And what's more, you'd have had him, too, if you'd never gone off for that holiday to Scarborough.

JENNY (*turning*). And met Arthur. (*She closes the drawer.*) I dare say you're right, Mother. (*Moving down a little.*) But, you see, I did go to Scarborough, and I did meet Arthur . . . And after I'd met him, neither Fred Whitworth nor anybody else mattered very much any more. (*She looks involuntarily towards the photograph.*)

MRS. COLLINS. Your cousin Bella was quick to seize her chance, anyway. She'd always wanted Fred—and now she's got him. Have I told you they're engaged ?

JENNY (*quietly*). Yes, Mother. (*To above the table.*) You've told me exactly four times since you arrived yesterday. I hope they'll be as happy as I am with Arthur—(*almost challengingly*) and that's saying a lot.

MRS. COLLINS. Oh, well, you'd no one to please but yourself, I suppose.

JENNY. I'd have liked to think you were pleased, too, Mother. It hurts me sometimes to—to feel you don't really like him.

MRS. COLLINS (*changing her position slightly*). I've said I've nothing against him.

JENNY. The trouble is, you don't try to understand him.

MRS. COLLINS. Are you so sure you understand him, yourself?

JENNY (*protestingly*). Why, of course I do!

MRS. COLLINS (*looking at her very directly*). You really feel—you *know* him—as well as one person can ever know another? There's no part of his life that's . . . hidden from you? You never . . . wonder?

JENNY (*her voice a shade higher*). What should I wonder?

MRS. COLLINS (*after a moment—not looking at* JENNY). Just who he is, and what he is!

JENNY (*a trace of impatience beginning to show in her tone*). He's Arthur Brown, tobacconist, aged forty-two, who married Jenny Collins, of Clapham, who loves and trusts him, Mother! *That's* who he is!

MRS. COLLINS (*about to say something further—then changing her mind*). All right, Jenny. We'll say no more.

JENNY (*with a sort of quiet determination*). Oh, yes, we will. (*Moving down* L. *of the table.*) We'll have this out, once and for all, if you don't mind.

MRS. COLLINS. Now, Jenny, please. I don't want you and me to quarrel.

JENNY. And we're not going to. Next to Arthur, you mean more to me than anyone else in the world, you know that.

(*With an impulsive gesture,* MRS. COLLINS *holds out her hand towards her daughter.* JENNY *takes it in hers.*)

MRS. COLLINS. It isn't that I don't *want* to like him, dear.

JENNY. I know that very well.

(*They release hands.*)

MRS. COLLINS. It's just that, somehow, I don't quite—you know—" *get* " him.

JENNY. *Get* him?

MRS. COLLINS. Let me try to tell you, Jenny . . . It always seems as though . . . part of him's . . . in shadow.—Yes, that's the word—shadow.

JENNY (*looking at her mother—after a moment*). You know, Mother, this is all imagination.

(Mrs. Collins *does not speak. A pause. Then, not looking at* Jenny, *she rises and goes down stage, below the table.*)

Mrs. Collins (*her back to* Jenny—*slowly*). Jenny ... why does he have to keep making these mysterious trips to Eastbourne ?

Jenny. There's nothing mysterious about it : it's to see his auntie, as you know.

Mrs. Collins. Even on your honeymoon, you had to come back two days earlier, because *he* must see his auntie.

Jenny. She couldn't help being taken worse, I suppose. (*Going to her mother.*) You know, you're making mountains out of molehills.

(*Instead of replying*, Mrs. Collins *moves to down* R. *Then :*)

Mrs. Collins (*facing her daughter now*). And why, when he does get back, must he have that haggard, nightmare look about him : as though he's been keeping company with ghosts and devils ? (*As* Jenny *starts to speak.*) The last time, when he walked in at that door, I hardly knew him. I didn't, really. His face all drawn, and he couldn't look at you when he spoke— not until he'd poured himself half a glass of neat whisky, and drunk it off. What had he been up to, to get in that state ?

Jenny. If you must know, he'd sat up all night with his auntie, to give the nurse a rest.

Mrs. Collins (*unconvinced*). Oh ?

Jenny. And he's always very kind to me when he gets back ; he always brings me a little present, always.

Mrs. Collins (*the words slipping out*). Conscience money !

Jenny. *Mother !*

Mrs. Collins (*quickly*). I'm sorry, Jenny. Pr'aps I shouldn't have said that.

Jenny. No, I don't think you should. (*She turns and goes towards the bureau.*) I've told you once, Mother, I *trust* him.

Mrs. Collins. So did she—till she found out—and it was too late.

Jenny (*moving down to just above the table*). Look here, Mother—you've got some queer fancy in your head ! What is it ? I want to know !

Mrs. Collins (*her back half-turned to* Jenny—*pretending to read*). I've told you : nothing.

(Jenny *comes down* L. *of her mother.*)

Jenny. What are you reading ? (*Looking over her mother's shoulder.*) " Wife-Strangler Pays the Penalty. Wainwright Hanged this Morning."

(Mrs. Collins *doubles the paper and drops it on to the table.*)

Why on earth d'you want to read such horrors ?

Mrs. Collins (*looking at her narrowly*). Don't you?
Jenny. I glanced at the case, but I couldn't bear it : it was horrible!
Mrs. Collins. Just . . . glanced at it? (*She is still looking at her. Then, very deliberately, she goes up* R.C., *to the bureau, opens the top drawer, and takes from it a little sheaf of newspaper-cuttings.*) I found these in this drawer yesterday, when we were hunting for your Uncle Edwin's photo. (*Moving down to below the* R.C. *chair.*) Someone in this house has been very interested in the Sevenoaks murder, it seems.
Jenny. What have you got there?
Mrs. Collins (*reading at random the headings of various cuttings*). "The Sevenoaks Murder Trial—Wainwright Gives Evidence—Gruelling Cross-Examination."
Jenny (*her voice just a little unsteady*). Why—Arthur must have cut them out.
Mrs. Collins (*reading more headings*). "Neighbours describe Wainwright as Mystery Man—Wainwright's Explanation of Trips to Sick Relative Exposed as Pack of Lies—Wainwright Found Guilty. Judge says, 'You wilfully deceived a wife who loved and trusted you, and when she discovered your true character, you butchered her in cold blood.'"
Jenny (*exclaiming*). Don't! (*Going quickly towards her mother—halting before she quite reaches her.*) So that's what you've been thinking! That Arthur—and that man—Arthur, who wouldn't hurt a fly——
Mrs. Collins (*reading from another heading*). "Witness speaks of Wainwright as most Tender-hearted Man he ever Met."
Jenny (*going right up to her mother—snatching the cuttings from her*). Give me those at once! (*She turns up to the bureau, stuffs them back into the drawer and slams it violently.*) You should be ashamed, Mother, to harbour such wicked thoughts!—I don't understand you!—*Aren't* you ashamed . . . downright ashamed?
Mrs. Collins (*who has crossed down* L.C.—*shaken by the other's reaction*). I'm sorry, Jenny, but—
Jenny (*to between the table and the chair* R.C.). To dare to suggest that Arthur—— What d'you suppose he'd say if he knew?—If I'd told him you'd—— It's dreadful, Mother, really dreadful!
Mrs. Collins. You don't suppose I've *wanted* to think such things?
Jenny. Comparing him to a beast of a man like that! A murderer! After all, just because I didn't marry the man you wanted me to, doesn't give you the right to blacken Arthur's character! He *is* your son-in-law, whether you like it or not.
Mrs. Collins (*soothingly*). I know, dear, I know. Now, please, Jenny——

JENNY. And what's more, he means everything in the world to me! Everything! I'm happy with him and I trust him! (*A little sobbing break in her voice.*) I trust him—always!

(*Her mother takes a step towards her, but* JENNY, *turning blindly, hurries to by the window, and sinks down on to the sofa. Her mother hesitates, then goes and sits beside her. There is a pause.* JENNY *gives a gulping sob, and makes a little dab at her eyes with her fingers, as though to flick the tears away.* MRS. COLLINS *takes a handkerchief which is tucked into her belt, and silently gives it to* JENNY. *The latter wipes her eyes, then hands it back to her mother.*)

MRS. COLLINS. I've said I'm sorry, dear, haven't I? . . . So let's be friends. (*A very short pause, then* JENNY *nods her head.*) That's right.

JENNY (*trying to control her voice*). Only—Mother—try to like him a little better. . . . He is my husband, you know.

(*Outside, in the yard, just beyond the window, a dog howls.* MRS. COLLINS *gives a start and a little exclamation.*)

MRS. COLLINS. Oh—that dog!

JENNY (*her lips trembling into a little half-smile*). Benjie. He howls like that sometimes when his master's away. . . . And when Arthur comes back, he'll hear him coming up the street. Out of all the other footsteps, he'll pick out Arthur's, and he'll bark. (*The dog howls again—rising—calling.*) Benjie! Benjie, be quiet! (*In her normal voice.*) He's heard me! He's wagging his tail! (*Calling again.*) Good dog! Master won't be long now! Good dog!

(*There is a knock at the door up* R., *which opens a little way to admit* MISS TASKER's *head.* MRS. COLLINS *has moved a little* L.)

MISS TASKER. Excuse me, Mrs. Brown, but there's a young lady and gentleman would like a word—a Mr. Whitworth and a Miss Crewe.

JENNY. Oh——

MRS. COLLINS. Fred and Bella! Well, I never! They've arrived!

JENNY (*to* MISS TASKER). Tell them to come in here, will you?

MISS TASKER. Very good. (*She withdraws her head, but does not close the door.*)

JENNY. Well, I'm glad you'll have company after all.

MRS. COLLINS (*flurriedly*). Jenny—listen—don't let them see there's been an upset!—You know what Bella is!

JENNY (*down* R.). Do I look——

MRS. COLLINS. You're all right. (*As* FRED *and* BELLA *enter.*) Why, Fred! Bella! This *is* nice of you!

(FRED WHITWORTH'S *appearance bears out* MRS. COLLINS'S *earlier description of him as a good, steady, young fellow, while* BELLA CREWE *is one of those under-brained and over-dressed little bits of femininity, who by some mysterious working of Providence, not infrequently succeed in securing one of the good, steady young fellows for their very own.*)

BELLA. Hullo, Auntie Grace! Did you think we weren't coming? We've had a lovely day! Hullo, Jenny! How are you? (*Hurrying to her.*) Let me look at you!—My dear, where did you get that dress? It makes you look ever so sallow!—I've got a new one, pink and white with touches of black. Fred says I look like a liquorice all-sort! Isn't he rude!
(*To* FRED, *who is below the table, shaking hands with* MRS. COLLINS.) Darling, where are your manners? Come and say "Hullo" to Jenny, here! Come on! (*To* JENNY.) You'll have heard about us, Jenny, I suppose?

(MRS. COLLINS *moves up* L. *of the table to above it.*)

FRED (*crossing* BELLA, *and shaking hands with* JENNY—*obviously pleased to see her*). Hullo, Jenny! Everything all right?
JENNY. Yes, thanks, Fred. And you?
BELLA (*on the* L. *of* FRED, *before he can reply*). You'll have heard we're engaged, Jenny? A week ago to-day!
JENNY. Yes. I hope you'll both be very happy.
FRED. Thank you, Jenny.
BELLA (*barely giving him time to get the words out*). We were sitting on the parlour sofa, and I was ever such a long time before I'd say Yes, wasn't I, Fred?—Oh, and I hear Bery Lomax is ever so cut up, and the Baxter boys, *and* a young man in our coal-merchant's office that I've never even spoken to! Isn't it a scream! (*She stuffs her handkerchief to her mouth, and giggles.*)
FRED (*hurriedly—to cut off her chatter*). And how's Arthur, Jenny? Gone to Eastbourne again, I hear.

JENNY. Yes. He's very well, thanks.

BELLA (*with a little toss of the head*). He wouldn't be very well if he was *my* husband and kept leaving me and careering off to Eastbourne! (*To* FRED.) So don't you go starting any invalid aunts, or *I'll* have something to say—won't I, Aunt Grace?

MRS. COLLINS (*forcing a smile*). I expect you would, Bella. But aren't you going to sit down?

BELLA (*moving to down* L.C.). Oh, we can't! We've got to catch the six-fifty back. . . . (*Turning to face* MRS. COLLINS.) If you're coming with us you'll have to look sharp and get your things on.

MRS. COLLINS. Well, I didn't want to leave until Arthur arrived.

JENNY. Of course you can, Mother. I'll be all right.

BELLA. Of course she will! She isn't a child! Tell me, Jenny, doesn't being married to a man as old as Arthur make you feel awfully old yourself?

JENNY. Arthur isn't exactly Methuselah, Bella. (*To* MRS. COLLINS.) Mother, do hurry, or you'll never catch that train.

MRS. COLLINS (*still doubtfully*). Well, if you really think . . .

JENNY (*decisively*). I'll be quite all right.

(*Somewhat reluctantly,* MRS. COLLINS *moves up* L., *towards the door.*)

BELLA. Can I come with you? I'd like to see upstairs! (*Starting to follow* MRS. COLLINS—*half-running—checking herself by the bureau.*) Oh, is this Arthur's photo? Oh, doesn't he look—— D'you know what Cissie Parker calls him, Jenny? Dark Brown! "And how's Dark Brown?" she says. "The Mystery Man!" (*She laughs, and starts again for the door—in the doorway.*) Oh, isn't this a gloomy room? D'you really like it, Jenny? I don't! Fred and me are going to have one of those new houses in Belvedere Terrace, aren't we, Fred?

FRED (*moving towards down* C.). All depends on the rent, milady.

BELLA. The rent's your business! And I do want a house with bow windows!

FRED. You'll be wanting one with a bathroom, next.

BELLA. What?—Oh, where's Auntie Grace? (*Rushing off.*) Auntie Grace! Auntie Grace! (*Off stage.*) Auntie Grace, where are you?

(*There is a very brief silence after she has gone. Now that* FRED *and* JENNY *are alone, they both feel slightly self-conscious and embarrassed.*)

FRED (*after clearing his throat—a jerk of his head towards the* L. *doorway*). I reckon Bella wasn't behind the door when tongues were given out, eh?

JENNY (*with a little smile*). No . . . Er—sit down, Fred, do.
FRED. Thanks.

(*He draws out the stiff-backed chair* R. *of the table, and sits.* JENNY *sits on the sofa. There is another brief pause. The following dialogue between the two should not flow too easily. There should be a barely perceptible little pause between each speech, until the one by* JENNY, *beginning* "London? That must have been . . ."*)

JENNY (*making conversation*). You're looking well, Fred.
FRED. I'm all right . . . I fancy you're looking a bit pale, though, Jenny.
JENNY. It must be the light. I'm feeling well enough.
FRED. And you're—happy, Jenny?
JENNY. Very happy, Fred.
FRED. That's all right, then.

(*A rather longer pause.*)

JENNY. You must come out again one day, when Arthur's at home.
FRED. Yes, I will. . . . I only met him that once, you know, at the wedding.
JENNY. He doesn't make friends easily. Some people think he's—queer, sort of—but he isn't a bit, really. It's just that he's very reserved.
FRED. Some men are like that, aren't they?
JENNY. I don't suppose you'd know him if you saw him, would you?
FRED. Matter of fact, I did see him one evening, in London.
JENNY. London? That must have been a good while ago.
FRED. No. It was the night of our office outing . . . let me see, a fortnight last Tuesday.
JENNY (*stiffening*). It couldn't have been. Arthur was in Eastbourne a fortnight last Tuesday.
FRED. Oh, but it was him—I'm positive.
JENNY (*rising abruptly*). In—*London*?
FRED (*blundering on*). In Leicester Square. He didn't see me, but I passed right close to him.
JENNY (*moving in to below the easy chair*). Fred!—are you sure?
FRED. 'Course I am.
JENNY (*a quick, barely audible intake of breath*). Oh!

(*She is holding herself absolutely rigid. He looks at her. Realizing that, somehow or other, he has blundered, his expression changes. He rises.*)

FRED (*concernedly*). Jenny—what's up? Aren't you well?
JENNY. It's nothing. I'm all right. (*She goes to down* R.)

FRED (*following her—standing behind her*). Look here—have I said something I shouldn't ? (*Her back to him—still quite rigid—she shakes her head.*) Jenny—what—— (*He puts his hand on her shoulder, as though to turn her round to face him.*) What's wrong ?

JENNY (*a shade louder—moving away a little*). Nothing.

(*There is a pause. It is now quite clear to* FRED *that his reference to the London encounter has been ill-chosen, and he racks his brain unhappily to conjure up means to repair the damage. Then :*)

FRED. If it's something I said just now . . . I've been thinking . . . and it wasn't a fortnight last Tuesday I was in London. It was three weeks. Yes—that's it—three weeks.

JENNY. Oh ? (*Turning to face him.*) But you couldn't have seen him then, either, for he was here, at home.

FRED (*weakly*). No, I couldn't, could I ? Well, I must have been mistaken. I only just caught a glimpse, you know.

JENNY. You're sure it was three weeks ago ?

FRED (*without any hesitation*). Positive.

JENNY (*still looking at him—after a pause*). I see.

FRED. It was silly of me, but——

JENNY. That's all right, Fred. (*Relaxing with an effort—with forced lightness.*) Not that it really mattered, of course.

FRED (*relaxing, too*). Mistakes will happen, eh ? (*A not very convincing little laugh.*)

JENNY. Sit down again, do, and let's talk about something else.

FRED. Thanks.

(*He moves back to the armchair* R. *of the table and is about to sit when the sound of* BELLA'S *voice is heard off stage. He remains standing.*)

Ah !

BELLA (*off stage*). Ma's so old-fashioned, you know ! You'd never believe ! Anything a bit smart, *she* thinks fast ! (*Entering, followed by* MRS. COLLINS.) But as I said to her yesterday, "When I'm married, I'll do as I like, and if I want to wear my hair in an Alexandra fringe, I will, and that's that."—(*Moving down to* JENNY, *who is by the sofa.*) Oh, Jenny, aren't those stairs narrow and dark ? And d'you really like that bedroom wallpaper ?—How are we for time, Fred ?

(MRS. COLLINS *is wearing her outdoor things, and is carrying a small bag.*)

FRED. We've none to waste. (*To* MRS. COLLINS, *going up, and taking her bag.*) Here, I'll take that.

MRS. COLLINS (*up* L.C.). Ta, Fred. (*Going to* JENNY.) You're sure you'll be all right, dear ?

JENNY. Of course.

(They kiss.)

BELLA *(crossing to him)*. Fred, your tie's worked all crooked! You do look a sight!—No, never mind it now, or we'll miss the train. Come on, Auntie! Bye-bye, Jenny!
FRED *(going to* JENNY—*shaking hands)*. Good-bye, Jenny.
JENNY. Good-bye, Fred.
BELLA *(impatiently)*. Good heavens, Fred! What d'you want to waste time shaking hands for? Anyone'd think you were never going to see Jenny again! Come on! *(As he joins her—the two moving towards the door up* R.*)* What shall I wear to-night? My moss green or my crushed strawberry?
FRED. I don't see it matters.
BELLA. Of course it matters!—Is this the way out?—

*(*FRED *opens the door—as they go out.)*

Of course it matters! Folk always stare so at a girl when she's just got engaged!—Come on, Auntie, come on!

(They go. MRS. COLLINS *does not immediately follow them. Instead, she puts her hands on her daughter's shoulders, and looks at her. Then:)*

MRS. COLLINS. If I've been a silly old woman, forgive me, Jenny.
JENNY. You're the best mother in the world.

(They kiss again.)

MRS. COLLINS *(her hands still on* JENNY'S *shoulders)*. Good-bye, dear.
JENNY *(forcing a little laugh)*. Why, you're as bad as Fred! You might never be going to see me again!—Good-bye, dear.

(Her mother releases her, touches her lightly on the cheek, then turns abruptly, and goes up stage and out, closing the door behind her. Left alone, JENNY *stands quite still for a moment, looking towards the door. Then, as though to shake off her thoughts, she starts to move about the room, smoothing the antimacassars, and straightening the cushions. Suddenly, she breaks off, goes to the bureau, opens the top drawer, takes out the little sheaf of cuttings, and starts to pore over them. . . . Daylight is just beginning to fade, and within the room, the shadows, which even at high noon are never utterly banished, are once more stealing forth to take possession. . . . There is a knock at the door, which opens to admit* MISS TASKER'S *head. At the sound of the knock,* JENNY *thrusts the cuttings back into the drawer.)*

MISS TASKER. Excuse me, but there's a lady asking to see you. Will you come out, or shall I . . .

JENNY. But—who is she?

MISS TASKER (*opening the door wider and admitting rather more of herself into the room*). A funny sort of name. Foreign, I'd say. . . . There's something a bit funny about the woman, too. I don't altogether . . .

JENNY. Oh—you'd better tell her to come in.

(MISS TASKER *withdraws, closing the door, but not latching it.* JENNY *shuts the drawer, and comes down a little, to just* R. *of the armchair by the fire.* MISS TASKER'S *voice is heard, off stage.*)

MISS TASKER'S VOICE. This way, please, and straight through.

(*The next moment, the door opens slowly, and there, framed in the doorway, is* MRS. PERSOPHELOUS. *A strange figure, indeed: tall, gaunt, and angular, wearing deep, flowing black, a veil of heavy black crepe concealing her features, and upon her hands, skin-tight gloves of chalk white.* JENNY *checks a little gasp, and stares at her. Then, moving to slightly below and* L. *of the table.*)

JENNY (*still staring*). You . . . wanted to see me?

(*Instead of replying, the woman raises her hands to her veil, lifts it and throws it back, revealing a face which is almost as dead-white as her gloves.*)

MRS. PERSOPHELOUS. You're Mrs. Brown, the wife of Arthur Brown?

JENNY. . . . Yes.

MRS. PERSOPHELOUS. Mr. Brown himself is not at home?

JENNY. No. He's . . .

MRS. PERSOPHELOUS (*moving down* R.C.). No matter. I happened to be nearby, and had a sudden whim to see him. I have business to attend to in London, and can stay but a moment, no more.

(*She sits in the armchair* R.C. *During the following short scene, she holds herself very stiff and upright, and makes occasional slow gestures with those white-gloved hands.*)

JENNY. Did you . . . want to see him particularly?
MRS. PERSOPHELOUS. Well, an aunt *should* see her nephew now and then, I fancy, eh?
JENNY (*staring at her—not speaking for a moment—then, as though scarcely believing her ears*). Aunt . . . did you say?
MRS. PERSOPHELOUS. By marriage, on the mother's side. Nowadays, the poor boy's only relative.
JENNY (*still staring—a step nearer*). Not . . . from Eastbourne?
MRS. PERSOPHELOUS. Eastbourne, certainly. I've been in residence there for many years—a very large house . . . But why do you stare at me like that? I must ask you not to, if you please. I don't like it at all.
JENNY. But—you've been ill, haven't you?
MRS. PERSOPHELOUS. Now, *how* do such rumours get abroad? I resent them very much. Ill, indeed! What next?
JENNY (*a little nearer*). But Arthur's been to see you—often! He has, hasn't he?
MRS. PERSOPHELOUS. I receive neither my nephew nor anyone. I live in complete retirement, and such is my rule. We may correspond occasionally. His last letter, I believe, was to tell me of his marriage to you. A charming girl, he said—and so you may be, but you stare too much, and that isn't nice, you know. So very rude.
JENNY. I'm sorry, but . . .
MRS. PERSOPHELOUS. Good manners are the flowers by the wayside of life. The humblest may pause and gather. I myself was lady's maid for many years to a very distinguished personage. More a friend than a maid, as she often remarked. We travelled abroad a great deal; and, in fact, I first met my husband by moonlight in Athens. Ill-met by moonlight, indeed. . . . You're still staring, I'm afraid. I'm beginning to regret this visit. It was impulsive of me. (*She rises.*)
JENNY (*taking a grip on herself—going quickly round the table, to* R. *of the armchair*). No, don't go—please!—There are things I want to know—must know—about Arthur—my husband.
MRS. PERSOPHELOUS. He is, I'm sure, a worthy man.
JENNY (*agitatedly—twisting her hands together*). But you say —he has *not* been to see you!
MRS. PERSOPHELOUS (*going slowly towards the window*). And my word can be accepted, I hope? (*Turning at the window.*) I've told you, I receive no one, save my counsellors and advisers —and then only at dead of night. (*Sinking down on to the sofa.*) Of course, it's entirely my own choice that I do not entertain more extensively. (*Extending a white-gloved hand towards the armchair* R.C., *graciously.*) You have my permission to sit.

(JENNY, *as though hypnotized, obeys.*)

The house is certainly big enough . . . with a pleasant garden, and very high walls. . . . But I cannot entirely approve the bars at the windows.

(JENNY *gives a little start, as her gathering suspicions are confirmed.*)

For a prison or a mad-house, yes; but for *my* house, I think not! . . . You agree?

JENNY (*faintly*). Yes . . . of course.

MRS. PERSOPHELOUS. They give one (*a gesture*) a shut-in feeling. . . . But all the same (*a look of cunning stealing over her face*), all the same—let me see—when was it—yesterday morning, I gave them the slip. (*A little laugh.*) Down the back stairs, out by the tradesmen's entrance, and off to the station. *That*'ll teach my women to gossip in corners, eh? Neglecting their duties! They'll be running round now, like frightened hens! (*Another little laugh which breaks off abruptly—looking round the room.*) What a very shadowy room this is! . . . But perhaps you don't mind shadows. . . . I quite like them, myself. (*Then—looking at* JENNY—*with a little puzzled frown.*) Let me see . . . who did you say you were?

JENNY (*shakily*). Your . . . nephew's wife.

MRS. PERSOPHELOUS. Nonsense. (*Shaking her head.*) I haven't got a nephew. I'm very much afraid, young woman, that you're an impostor.

JENNY (*rising*). You mean—you're not Arthur Brown's aunt?

MRS. PERSOPHELOUS. Arthur Brown? The name tastes like mud in the mouth! Do I look like the aunt of an Arthur Brown? Because if I do, then one thing's *very* clear: I must change my milliner at once!

JENNY. But—you called here to see Arthur, didn't you?

MRS. PERSOPHELOUS (*frowning again*). *I* did? Certainly not! Ridiculous! And what's more, I've other things to think about! (*Slightly louder.*) If I'm to claim my rights, I mustn't be idling here! (*Rising.*)

(JENNY *rises also, backing a little* L.)

By this time to-morrow, young woman, history will have been made! The whole thing is to be thrashed out after dinner to-night at the Palace! She and I! Woman to woman! Good-bye. (*Starting towards the door up* R., *then pausing.*) I've decided to let her keep Balmoral. I should never survive those Highland draughts. But on every other point, I'm adamant! (*Going to the door—turning—standing in the doorway—appearing to think for a moment—then, her manner much more normal.*) *What* was the name you mentioned? . . . Arthur Brown? . . . (*Moving down a little.*) But, of course, my nephew! . . .

My dear, you must forgive me! My memory, it comes and goes!—And Arthur!—How is he?—I'd have liked to see him!

JENNY (*going quickly nearer to her—anxiously*). Are you so sure you *haven't* seen him—very recently? (*Almost pleadingly.*) *Please* try to remember!

MRS. PERSOPHELOUS (*shaking her head—emphatically*). Seen him? . . . No! . . . (*Then—her manner " clouding over " again—drawing herself up—very imperiously.*) Tell him, if you please, that his aunt, the Princess Sophia Frederica Anastasia, called. . . . I wish you good evening.

(*Raising her hands, she lowers her veil, turns, and goes. . . .*
JENNY *does not move. Then she takes a few hurried steps, as though to call the other back, halts abruptly in the doorway, pauses there, then turns to face into the room. She looks quickly round the room, as though it has somehow undergone some subtle change. Her look rests finally upon the armchair. She takes a few steps towards it, then checks herself at a sound from outside.* MISS TASKER *comes hurrying in.*)

MISS TASKER (*excitedly*). Oh, Mrs. Brown—excuse me—but whoever is she, the lady who's just gone out?

JENNY (*hesitating*). I don't know——

MISS TASKER. There's something—funny about her, isn't there? I couldn't make her out at all! She really frightened me! . . . And the way she's gone off down the street! I watched her! Bowing to left and to right—like Royalty. You should see folk stopping and staring!—If you ask me, *her* proper place is a mad-house!

JENNY. . . . Yes.

MISS TASKER. I'd never have let her in to you, if I'd known. You're looking ever so white.

JENNY (*striving to keep her voice quite calm*). I'm all right.

MISS TASKER. Oh, well, Mr. Brown'll be back any minute now, eh? (*Going towards the door.*) It's been a creepy sort of evening altogether, what with her, and every blessed customer harping on this Wainwright man. It's funny, isn't it, how one particular murder, every now and then, seems to catch folk's fancy?

JENNY. He . . . deceived his wife, didn't he?

MISS TASKER (*with a nod*). And murdered her when she found out. They say he'd been suspecting she might find out, and he carried the rope about with him in a little bag, just in case. And what *I* say is, it's a pity *she* didn't carry a gun!

JENNY. A gun?

MISS TASKER. I'm sure, after what a tobacconist shop's taught me of men, if I was ever such a fool as to think of marrying one, I'd buy up half Woolwich Arsenal as part of my trousseau. (*Then, adding quickly.*) Not that there mayn't be *some* good men

—Mr. Brown, for instance, and, of course, the late Prince Albert. But two swallows hardly make a summer, do they, Mrs. Brown ? (*Outside, in the yard, the dog commences to bark.*) There, now ! There *is* Mr. Brown ! Benjie hears him coming up the street ! —I'd better nip back behind the counter, quick, or I'll be getting the sack !

(*She hurries out, leaving the door wide open. At the sound of the dog's bark,* JENNY'S *whole body has stiffened. She stands tense and taut, her arms straight down at her sides, her head just a little up-tilted, as though listening for the sound of footsteps. . . . Then, suddenly, she looks towards the bureau. The next instant she has crossed to the bureau, snatched up the photograph, and is staring at it. The "ting" of the shop-bell is heard. She thrusts the photograph back, giving a quick look towards the door as she does so. Then she crosses quickly to the fireplace, and stands there, waiting. There is a quite appreciable pause. Then* ARTHUR BROWN *appears in the passage outside. He is a rather heavily-built man, slightly above average height, in his early middle age. His hair is beginning to grey at the sides, and his expression appears to betray some signs of strain or tiredness—or both. He is carrying his hat and a small bag, and his coat is slung over his arm. There is that in his manner which suggests that he has had a pretty rough upbringing, and when he speaks, it is with a faint North Country accent.*)

ARTHUR (*in the passage—not immediately noticing her*). Jen' ! Where—oh, you're there, are you ? (*Coming into the room.*) I didn't see you at first. (*He places his hat and coat upon one of the stiff-backed chairs up stage, then goes to the table and sets his bag down on it.*) Well, I'm here—back again !

JENNY. Yes, Arthur.

ARTHUR (*to* L. *of the table*). Glad to see me, eh, Jen' ?

JENNY (*he is standing very close to her now—directly in front of her*). Aren't I always glad to see you when you come back from . . . Eastbourne.

ARTHUR. That's right. (*He puts his hands on her shoulders and kisses her. She is completely unresponsive.*) Here, I say !

What's this ? A blooming iceberg ? (*She hesitates, then bends her head forward, and kisses him.*) You can do better than that, too, I reckon, but it'll do to be going on with. (*Releasing her.*) Where's your ma, eh ? (*He is crossing towards down* R.)

JENNY. She went back early, with Cousin Bella and Fred Whitworth. They were down for the day.

ARTHUR (*opening the cupboard door down* R., *and taking out a bottle of whisky and a glass*). Fred ? The young chap who was sweet on you before I came on the scene, eh ? How is he ?

JENNY. All right. (*Striving to speak quite casually.*) He was saying he saw you in London, a fortnight last Tuesday.

(*He was just about to pour the whisky, but at this he pauses, the bottle poised over the glass.* JENNY *is watching him very closely.*)

ARTHUR (*after the pause*). Saw me ? He couldn't have. I was in Eastbourne then, with Auntie.

JENNY. That's what I said. (*He pours the drink, the bottle clinking slightly against the glass as he does so.*) Your hand's trembling, isn't it, Arthur ?

ARTHUR (*replacing the bottle in the cupboard*). I shouldn't wonder—after sitting up all night. (*He takes a fairly long drink. Then, crossing to* R.C., *rather obviously changing the subject.*) Why don't you sit down, Jen' ? You look funny, standing there like that.—Oh, but I'm forgetting ! I've got a little present for you, Jen' ! (*He puts the glass down on the table.*) A present from Eastbourne. (*Going to her—taking a string of beads from his jacket-pocket.*) Beads ! (*Holding them up.*) Like 'em ?

JENNY (*in a very controlled voice—making no move to take them*). Thank you, Arthur. They're very nice.

ARTHUR. Let's see how they look on.

(*He takes the beads in both hands, and is about to clasp them round her neck. Her body stiffens.*)

JENNY (*as his hands almost touch her neck—suddenly—wildly—seizing both his hands and thrusting them from her*). No ! No !—Take your hands away !—*Don't touch me !—Don't !*

ARTHUR (*startled*). Here ! Here, I say ! What on earth——

JENNY (*hastily*). I'm sorry, I—(*lamely*) I thought you were—going to play a trick on me, or something.

ARTHUR (*staring at her*). Play a trick ?

JENNY. It was silly of me. Give me the beads. They're very nice.

(ARTHUR *hesitates, still looking at her somewhat uncertainly, then holds out the beads in silence. She takes them and starts to clasp them round her throat.* MISS TASKER, *wearing a hat and jacket, appears in the doorway up* R.)

Miss Tasker. Oh—excuse me, please—I'm going now, Mr. Brown.
Arthur (*moving above the table*). That's all right. I'll lock up after you.
Miss Tasker. Good night, then. Good night, Mrs. Brown.
Jenny. Good night.
Miss Tasker (*on the point of going*). Er—any better news of your auntie, Mr. Brown ?
Arthur (*taking his glass from the table*). Just about the same.
Miss Tasker. Just about the same. Oh dear !

(*She goes.* Arthur *drinks, replaces his glass on the table, and goes towards the doorway up* R.)

Jenny (*a sharp "nervy" edge to her voice*). Where are you going ?
Arthur. Lock up.

(*He goes out. For a moment she does not move. Then, suddenly, her self-control snaps. Her hands fly to her throat, and, as though the beads are choking her, she drags them off, and swings round as though to drop them on to the mantelshelf. There is the sound from off stage of the rattle of keys, and of a heavy bolt being pushed home. She pauses ; then, as the sounds cease, she drops the beads on to the mantelshelf, and moves quickly away from the fireplace, to just above the table. As she does so,* Arthur *returns. He goes straight to the table, picks up his glass, and drinks. He is about to take another drink, when he catches her eye, pauses, and stares at her.*)

Jen'—what are you staring at me like that for ? What's up ? Is anything . . . wrong ?
Jenny. I . . . don't know.
Arthur. You don't know ? What d'you mean ? (*He puts his glass down on the table, and goes right up to her.*) There *is* something wrong, isn't there ? (*Her lips move, but she does not speak. He moves as though to put his hand on her arm.*) See here, Jen'——
Jenny (*drawing back—sharply*). No ! !
Arthur. Jen' !
Jenny (*pointing*). Go over there, by the window !
Arthur. What ?
Jenny (*still pointing*). I'll not utter another word, Arthur— not another—till you do as I say !
Arthur. But—— (*He looks at her a second longer. Then :*) Oh, all right, then. (*He turns, and crosses towards the window. As he reaches it, the dog in the yard, seeing him, begins to bark. He goes to the window, and shouts.*) Shut up, Benjie ! Stop your row, will you ! Shut up ! (*The barking ceases, and he closes the window, then faces her again.*) Now then, what's all this about ?

What's riled you ? Is it your mother been making trouble ?
Or that Fred What's-'is-name who pretended he saw me in London
when I was God knows how many miles away ? (*As she does not
immediately speak.*) Eh ?

JENNY (*very meaningly*). Are you so very sure he didn't see
you ?

ARTHUR (*with just a hint of bluster*). Don't be so daft, Jen' !
How could I be in two places at once ?

JENNY. Some folk can.

ARTHUR. Eh ?—Look here, Jen', just what are you getting at ?

JENNY. Your auntie—she can be bedridden in Eastbourne
—and be here at the same time ! (*Louder.*) Here, in this
room ! (*Pointing.*) Sitting in that chair ! (*On a slightly
hysterical note.*) Your auntie ! From the mad-house ! Eastbourne !

(*Her voice snaps off. There is a long silence. At her words, his
whole body has frozen into stillness. She is half the width of the
room away from him, is looking at him accusingly, and he must
force himself to meet that look. He runs his tongue over his lips.
His lips move. But no words come.*)

(*Quieter.*) You can't think of anything to say to me now, can
you ? This is the minute you've always dreaded might happen !
I know !

(*A shorter pause. Then :*)

ARTHUR (*forcing the words*). She's been here ? (*His hand
strays to his jacket pocket. He withdraws a telegram.*)

JENNY (*after one slow nod*). Even the cleverest of liars and
deceivers get found out . . . sometimes.

(*An even shorter pause.*)

ARTHUR (*very quietly*). I knew she was missing. I got this
yesterday. . . . I reckon there's naught to be done but to tell
you. . . . She was always a bit queer, they say. . . . Big
ideas. . . . And she went as maid to a titled lady, who took
a fancy to her, and educated her a bit and took her about. . . .
And then, she married a foreign chap—and he wasn't much good
—and it made her queerer than ever—until she got so she had
to be put away.

JENNY. But it wasn't part of her queerness when she said
she hadn't set eyes on you for years . . . was it ? (*Louder.*)
Was it ?

ARTHUR. . . . No, Jen'. I thought this might happen.
(*Then, a little louder.*) I'd have given anything not to have gone
—this time.

JENNY (*bitterly*). Yes, I dare say you would—after tricking
me into marrying you !

ARTHUR. Nay, now, I used no tricks. (*Starting to move towards her.*) I courted you as honest and open as I could.

JENNY (*a gesture to him to come no nearer*). No!

(ARTHUR *halts a little to* R. *of the table. She looks at him, seems about to speak, then goes and sits in the easy chair. A very short pause.*)

(*On the edge of the chair—bolt upright—not looking at him, but directly in front of her.*) It's not for nothing that they call you "Dark Brown" . . . for it's just what you are. . . . You come from somewhere up North. Nobody knows anything about you—or your folk—if you've got any. And you set yourself up as a respectable shopkeeper, and it all *looks* all right. . . . But it isn't, is it? No! There's a something *wrong* about you. Something not quite . . . And everybody, even my own mother, can sense it. . . . Everybody but me—and I'm fool enough to *marry* you! And to *trust* you! Oh, my God!

ARTHUR (*almost pleadingly*). Jen', listen : don't say any more now : wait till to-morrow.

JENNY. No! We've got to have this out *now*! I want to know *now*, just what it is I'm tied to! (*Turning towards him.*) This morning, in London, they hanged a man like you!

ARTHUR (*quietly—but with a sudden firmness*). Shut up, Jen'.

JENNY. Just such a one as you! Wainwright, the strangler! (*Springing up—pointing to the bag.*) Is it there in your bag? The rope?

ARTHUR (*a quick step forward—as though the word "rope" has stung him—his hands clenched at his sides—much louder*). Will you shut up! I've asked you once, and I mean it, d'you hear? Shut up! Shut *up*!

(*Just for a moment she is afraid. She flinches and draws back a step. Then :*)

JENNY (*her voice not quite steady*). I'm not afraid of you, Arthur. I won't let myself be.

ARTHUR. Then let's have no more play-actress talk of ropes and such. . . . I loved you, and married you, and treated you decent. What more d'you want?

JENNY (*a step towards him*). The truth. You've told me lies, and I want to know the truth! I've *got* to know the truth now!——

(*Her voice breaks off. She presses the back of her hand to her mouth for a second, then goes to down* L., *and stands there, her back to him. A short pause. Then he moves round the back of the table, and down towards her, halting a little behind and to* R. *of her. When he speaks, he does so quite quietly, and as though weighing every word.*)

ARTHUR. All right, Jen', I've lied to you—*because I had to.* . . . Will you just let it go at that, and say no more ?

(JENNY *shakes her head.*)

Jen' !

JENNY. No.

(ARTHUR *puts out his hand and takes one of hers in his. She snatches it away, and swings round to face him.*)

Where did you go when you left me yesterday ? And all those other times ! Where did you go ? Where ?

(ARTHUR *does not speak for a moment. Then :*)

ARTHUR. On business.
JENNY. Your business is out there, in the shop.
ARTHUR. A side-line. Something you know nothing about. (*Very earnestly.*) Jen', don't ask any more !
JENNY. Side-line ? (*He looks at her dumbly, almost appealingly.*) No, Arthur, I've *got* to know !

(*A very short pause.*)

ARTHUR (*haltingly*). My father . . . he was a shoemaker . . . up North. . . . But *he* was something else, too. . . . He had the side-line. . . . I was brought up to think of it as (*a little shrug*) just a job to be done. . . . But now—since we've been married—it's begun to get me down—I knew I couldn't go on with it—and I chucked it. To-day was the last time. There'd have been no more trips to Eastbourne, Jen'.
JENNY. You're talking riddles—trying to put me off. What is this side-line ?
ARTHUR. I've told you—just a job to be done.
JENNY. But—something you couldn't tell me ?
ARTHUR (*with a sort of irritated weariness*). No—no, I couldn't.
JENNY (*persisting*). Something that—if I'd known—I'd never have married you ?
ARTHUR (*as before*). P'r'aps—p'r'aps not. (*Turning away—going towards up stage.*) Damn it, I don't know. (*Then, under his breath.*) Oh, my God ! (*Turning towards her again.*) Listen, Jen', listen : whatever I've done or been, it's all over and finished. Can't you be satisfied with that ? I've done you no wrong, I give you my word.
JENNY. *Your word !* (*Starting towards him—halting halfway —slowly.*) His way was best ! Wainwright ! He killed quickly, with a rope—not slowly, with words !

(*Once again it is as though the word " rope " has stung him. For a second he does not move. He just looks at her. The next instant, his look—everything about him, in fact—is transformed,* as though every vestige of self-control has suddenly been swept away on a tide of blind fury. She sees the swift change, but before she has time to react, he springs at her and seizes her by the shoulders.)

ARTHUR (*shaking her violently—shouting*). What d'you want to keep on about him for ?—I told you to shut up, didn't I ?—D'you want to drive me mad ?—I won't have it, damn you !—I won't have it, d'you hear ?—I *won't* have it ! !

(*He thrusts her from him. She staggers and collapses back into the easy chair, and cowers back into the corner of it, staring up at him, her face contorted with fear. In two swift striding steps he is beside the chair, every muscle taut, his fists pressed to his chest, his breath coming hissingly between his clenched teeth. His body bends a little towards her, and she thrusts out her hands, as though to ward him off. He straightens himself, gives a little shake of his head, as though to clear his thoughts, then suddenly turns, dashes to the door up* L., *and goes out, slamming the door behind him. At the sound of the slam she sits bolt upright, her hands gripping the sides of the chair. Then, with a choking exclamation, she springs up and half-runs towards the door which leads to the shop. Before she quite reaches it, he returns, carrying her hat and jacket. Going straight to her, up* R.C., *he thrusts them into her hands.*)

(*Holding himself in check—gruffly.*) Here, take these, and get back to your mother !—We're finished !—Your other things'll be sent along !—I'll see you're all right for money !—Only go now !——

JENNY (*suddenly no longer afraid—clutching the hat and jacket to her—staring at him*). Arthur . . . what . . .

ARTHUR (*much more quietly—and, above all, quite undramatically*). I hanged George Wainwright. . . . D'you understand now ?

(*At first his words do not seem to penetrate. Then :*)

JENNY (*stunned*). . . . You ? (*She backs a little down* R.)

ARTHUR (*still quite undramatically*). This morning—before it was quite light—at Pentonville—I hanged him.

(*A silence. Then :*)

JENNY (*never taking her eyes off him*). So that's what . . .

ARTHUR (*with a quick nod—brusquely—as though determined to banish all sentiment and feeling*). I told you, didn't I, a sideline ? A job that someone's got to do. First my father—then me. (*Dropping his voice slightly.*) So now you know. (*With a flick of his hand towards her hat and jacket.*) Reckon you'd better get your things on. You couldn't stay here with me now. . . . (*As she continues to stare at him.*) Well ? Why don't you . . .

JENNY (*as though rooted to the spot—dazedly—weakly*). I—don't—know.

(*Still staring at him, her hands, the one holding her hat, the other her jacket, fall limply to her sides. She remains like that for a moment, then she turns slowly towards the window, the jacket trailing along the floor. From this point, to the end of the play, the whole thing should be taken quite slowly and quite quietly, with full value given to the pauses.*)

(*By the window.*) . . . I don't know.

(*She drops the hat and jacket haphazardly on to the sofa, then sits. A pause. He watches her, hesitates, then moves down L. of the armchair to beside her. Another pause.*)

ARTHUR (*unsteadily—as though afraid to sound too eager*). Jen', you don't mean—you don't think—— (*His voice breaks off.*)

(*A short pause.*)

JENNY (*not looking at him*). It's funny, but, all at once, everything seems to have gone very quiet and still. . . . I can even hear the clock ticking out there in the kitchen. (*A pause. Then, looking at him—speaking in a quite normal, almost matter-of-fact voice.*) I shall stay here, Arthur. This is my home.

ARTHUR (*not able to speak for a second—then, very softly*). Oh . . . Jen'.

(*With a clumsy movement he drops to his knees beside her, and makes a move as though to put his arms round her.*)

JENNY (*laying her hand quite gently on his shoulder—checking his move—with a barely perceptible shake of her head*). No, Arthur. . . . One day, perhaps. . . . But not yet . . . not just yet.

There is a further pause, while they both remain quite still. **And then—**

The CURTAIN *slowly falls.*

OTTERY ST. MARY, DEVONSHIRE.
June, 1945.

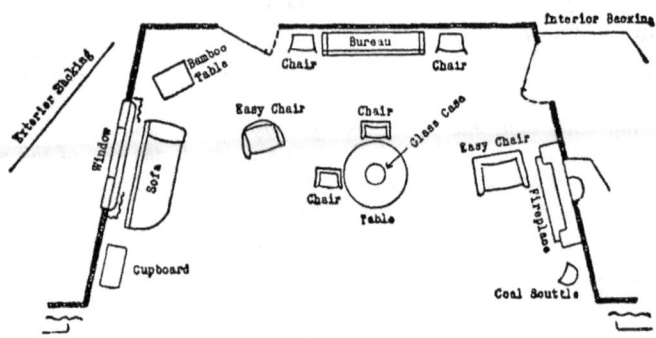

FURNITURE AND PROPERTY PLOT

Carpet on stage.
Rug at hearth.
Lace curtains at window, looped with satin.
Heavier curtains in addition to the above (maroon).
On the Walls.—Several pictures (landscape reproductions).
  2 or 3 plaques.
  2 Japanese fans.
  2 fretwork brackets, with small vases.
On the Mantel.—1 tall vase with pampas grass.
  2 bronze equestrian figures.
  Various small ornaments.
  A clock.
1 sofa (late nineteenth century).
1 armchair (at fire, in velvet).
4 stiff-backed chairs to match armchair.
1 large easy chair (in distinctive bright colour).
1 small bamboo table.
  On it.—A plant.
1 large round table.
  On it.—Fringed tablecloth.
    Domed glass case of wax fruit and flowers.
  (*Note.*—Antimacassars on all chairs and sofa.)
1 large cupboard (down R.).
  In it.—Whisky-bottle and glass.
1 bureau, or sideboard (up C.).
  On it.—Biscuit barrel.
    Fruit bowl.
    Framed photograph.
  In drawer of same.—Several newspaper cuttings.
Fireirons, coal scuttle, screen in front of fire.

PERSONAL PROPERTIES.

MRS. COLLINS.—Newspaper, reading magnifying-glass.
JENNY.—(*1st entrance*)—Apron.
  (*2nd entrance*)—Vase of fresh flowers.
BELLA.—Small handbag.
FRED.—Straw hat ("boater").

Mrs. Collins.—(*2nd entrance*)—Small suitcase.
Arthur.—Small bag ; bead necklace in coat pocket.
(*2nd entrance*)—Jenny's hat and coat.
Miss Tasker.—(*Final entrance*)—Hat and jacket.

LIGHTING PLOT

To Open.—Floats : Amber and pink ¾, white ¼.
Battens : Amber and pink FULL, white ½.
Straw flood on exterior cloth.
Amber lengths on interior backings.

Cue 1.—*As* Mrs. Collins *and* Bella *re-enter*—Commence slow check of white in floats to *nil*, and in battens to ¼. (*Complete this check as* Jenny *pores over the newspaper cuttings.*)

Cue 2.—*When Cue* 1 *is complete*—Slowly change straw flood to No. 4 amber. Follow with No. 4 amber flood through windows. across L.C. chair to up R

Cue 3.—Miss Tasker. ". . . quick, or I'll be getting the sack." (*Exit.*) —Check white in battens to *nil*. Amber in floats to ½.

Cue 4.—*After* Arthur *exits for* Jenny's *hat and coat*—Slowly check all in floats and battens by a quarter. *When* Arthur *returns*—Slow check of all in floats, to *nil* (30 seconds).

www.ingramcontent.com/pod-product-compliance
Lightning Source LLC
Chambersburg PA
CBHW061518040426
42450CB00008B/1684